Eric The Red
and
Leif The Lucky

by Barbara Schiller
illustrated by Hal Frenck

Troll Associates

Troll Associates

Library of Congress Catalog Card Number: 78-18055
ISBN 0-89375-174-X
ISBN 0-89375-166-9 Paper Edition

10   9   8   7   6   5   4   3   2

Eric The Red
and
Leif The Lucky

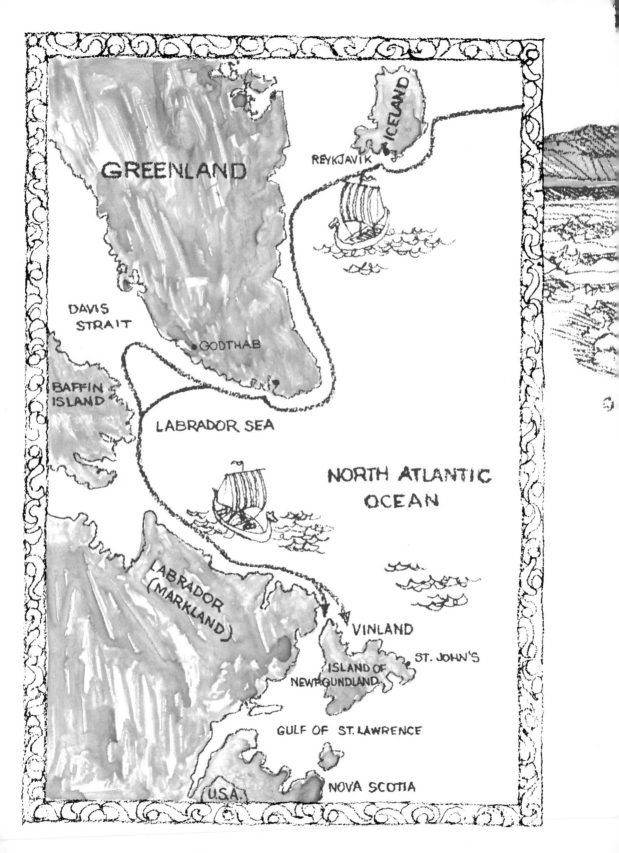

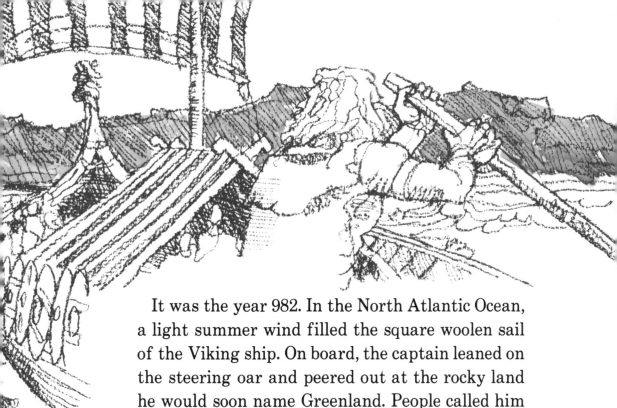

It was the year 982. In the North Atlantic Ocean, a light summer wind filled the square woolen sail of the Viking ship. On board, the captain leaned on the steering oar and peered out at the rocky land he would soon name Greenland. People called him Eric the Red because of the long red hair that reached almost to his shoulders.

Eric, a tall, bearded Norseman in his thirties, had sailed from his home in Iceland several days before. With him were his wife and three young sons, about forty followers, and some livestock.

All his life, Eric had heard tales of a land to the west of Iceland. He had often longed to sail there and explore. Now the bow of his ship was slicing through the cold waters toward Greenland's strange shores.

Eric was like most Vikings—not content to stay at home. These tall, fair-haired people had always been adventurers and fierce warriors. They were also daring and skillful sailors who journeyed far from their native Scandinavia in long, swift "dragon ships." Many of them settled in Iceland. From here they often raided the coasts of England, France, and Germany. Armed with double-edged swords, heavy spears, and battle-axes, they kept the people of Western Europe in constant terror.

6

Eric the Red was a skilled seaman and a born leader. The men who had volunteered to sail with him to Greenland trusted him fully—or they would not have come. But they also knew that Eric could be hot-tempered. A few months earlier, he had killed a man in a fight. For this, he had been banished from Iceland.

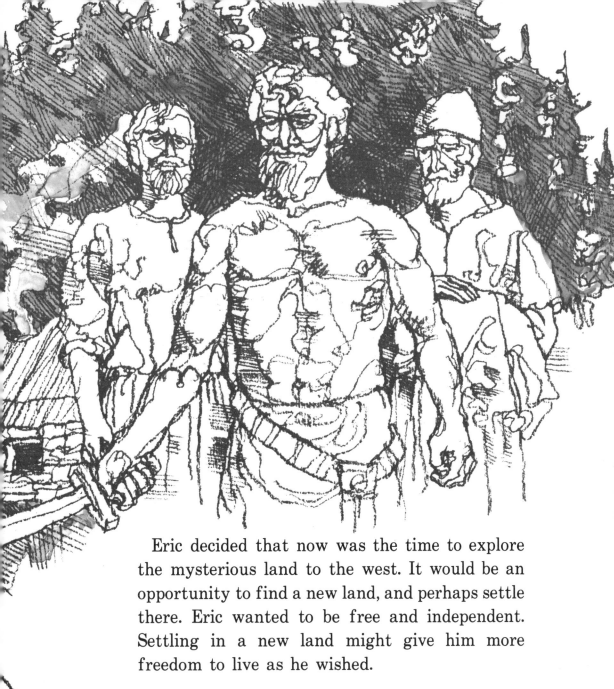

Eric decided that now was the time to explore the mysterious land to the west. It would be an opportunity to find a new land, and perhaps settle there. Eric wanted to be free and independent. Settling in a new land might give him more freedom to live as he wished.

9

Even though it was summer, Eric and his followers found the eastern coast of Greenland clogged with ice. Everybody aboard knew how short the summers were in the northern climate. They knew they had to find a place to land and build shelter before winter came.

Eric sailed his ship around the southern tip of this lonely land and headed up the western coast. It was a long sail, and the winds were wild. It took all of his skill to bring the vessel through safely.

Finally, the ship came to a region of fjords and many offshore islands. Like fingers from the sea, the fjords were long, narrow inlets of water between steep cliffs. On one of the islands, Eric and his men found the hunting and fishing extremely good. It was here that the adventurers decided to spend their first winter. Eric named the island *Ericholm*—Eric's Home.

10

With the coming of spring, Eric once again took to his ship. He explored the fjords. There were many with rocky cliffs. But some had sloping banks with long stretches of green grass and flowering hillsides.

One day, Eric showed his wife a very long fjord. Its upper banks were especially beautiful. There was a sparkling stream and dark green pastures protected by low hills. "I will call this place Eric's Fjord," he said.

"We shall make our home here," said his wife.

During the next three summers, Eric led his followers up most of the fjords, and explored the islands that dotted the southern coastline of Greenland. He gave names to many places. He believed that this region would be good for hunting, farming, and grazing animals. The climate reminded him of Iceland. "Here," Eric told his wife, "we can be free. It is *better* than Iceland!"

Eric began to make his plans for the future. This uninhabited land was ready for settlers. He decided to go to Iceland and bring back more people, animals, and supplies. He also decided to name the entire land *Greenland*. This name would appeal to farmers looking for fertile land and good pastures for their cattle.

15

When Eric returned to Iceland, there were many
people willing to listen to him. They admired his
fine cargo of Greenland reindeer, seal, and walrus
hides. They also saw that all of Eric's followers
were in good health. Greenland, they agreed, must
be a wonderful place.

16

A terrible famine had swept Northern Europe a few years earlier. Many farmers in Iceland were still poor and hungry. They were eager to go with Eric the Red to this new country, where he said there would be no shortage of food or land.

17

In the spring of 985, Eric again set out for Greenland. This time, he sailed with twenty-five ships loaded with settlers, supplies, and livestock.

18

The voyage was difficult and stormy. Towering waves and strong winds battered the ships. Some of the ships were forced to turn back to Iceland. Others sank, and people died. When land came into view at last, only fourteen ships and 350 people were left.

The survivors settled along the fjords of southwest Greenland. Since there were no trees for lumber, they built houses of stone and sod. They began to raise cattle, sheep, and horses. It wasn't long before others arrived from Iceland to start a second settlement, farther north.

The new Greenlanders lived much as they had in Iceland. But now they were almost totally dependent on trade. Such things as wheat, lumber, and linen had to be imported.

Because this trade was so necessary, a new breed of adventurers sprang up among the Greenlanders. They risked their lives roving the wild waters of the North Atlantic. In their ships, they carried furs, hides, and rope to trade for the necessities of life on Greenland.

As the years passed, Eric the Red watched his son, Leif, become an expert sailor and a daring explorer. At first, Leif sailed under other captains. Then he was given ships of his own to command. Leif Ericson made many voyages between Greenland, Scotland, Iceland, and Norway.

Sometimes the aging Eric feared that his son would not return from his voyages. But always the smiling, bearded Leif Ericson, his ship battered by bad weather, made it safely back to Greenland. Luck seemed to go with him wherever he went. People began to call him "Leif the Lucky."

As was the custom, Leif spent his winters in his father's house. He played chess, listened to songs and music, and heard exciting *sagas*—long adventure stories—about the deeds of heroic Vikings. What tales they were!

One winter he heard a young seafarer, named Bjarni Herjulfsson, tell of sighting a strange new land far to the west of Greenland.

22

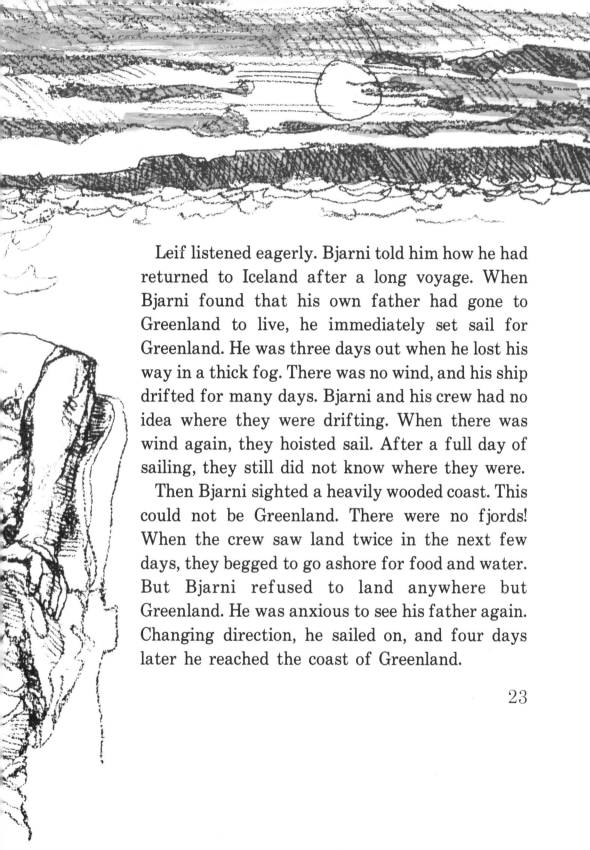

Leif listened eagerly. Bjarni told him how he had returned to Iceland after a long voyage. When Bjarni found that his own father had gone to Greenland to live, he immediately set sail for Greenland. He was three days out when he lost his way in a thick fog. There was no wind, and his ship drifted for many days. Bjarni and his crew had no idea where they were drifting. When there was wind again, they hoisted sail. After a full day of sailing, they still did not know where they were.

Then Bjarni sighted a heavily wooded coast. This could not be Greenland. There were no fjords! When the crew saw land twice in the next few days, they begged to go ashore for food and water. But Bjarni refused to land anywhere but Greenland. He was anxious to see his father again. Changing direction, he sailed on, and four days later he reached the coast of Greenland.

23

Leif Ericson could not understand why Bjarni had shown so little curiosity about the new land he had sighted. Others, too, hearing the tale, vowed to find and explore this far-off land for themselves. None was more determined to make this westward voyage of discovery than Leif Ericson.

But Leif needed a ship of his own. So he bought Bjarni's ship and hired a crew of thirty-five experienced sailors, including some of Bjarni's original crew. Then he began to outfit his new ship with everything necessary for a long sea voyage... and a hard winter ashore in a strange land.

24

An ocean-going Viking ship of Leif Ericson's time was about 23 meters (75 feet) long. It usually carried one small boat aboard and towed another behind. The sixteen pairs of oars were used only when there was no wind, or for maneuvering in shallow waters. This well-designed ship, with its long, full keel, could be steered easily in the roughest seas. When the wind and weather were good, it could cover over 160 kilometers (100 miles) in a single day.

As the time for his departure drew near, Leif Ericson asked his father to join him. Once again, Eric the Red thought about leading an expedition of discovery. He wanted to go . . . but he told his son he was too old. How could he endure the hardships of such a voyage? But Leif asked him again and again. At last, Eric the Red agreed to go.

When the ship was ready to sail, father and son rode down toward the shore on horseback. Suddenly, the father's horse stumbled, throwing him to the ground. He was not hurt. But he looked at his son sadly.

"This is as far as we go together," he said. "It would be foolish to ignore this sign from the gods. I am not fated to discover more countries than the one we now live in."

Leif smiled and shook his father's hand. He was sad to leave Eric behind, but he understood and respected his father's decision.

26

Leif Ericson and his crew members boarded the ship. Each man carried his belongings in a sea chest. Among the sailors was Tyrkir, an old and trusted servant of his father's. Tyrkir had been his good friend as long as he could remember, and Leif was glad to have him along.

28

When the crew had made the ship ready, they hoisted the single woolen sail and put out to sea. It was spring of the year 1001. The wind was favorable, and the currents were with them. The crew believed this proved that luck was on their captain's side.

Leif Ericson had carefully planned this voyage. As he handled the steering oar, his eyes searching the horizon, he wondered what adventures and hardships lay ahead.

For several days the Viking ship sailed westward, pushed by a strong breeze. In that time, there were no compasses to guide sailors. A captain had to steer largely by the stars. Nevertheless, Leif Ericson sailed well. When land was finally sighted, he brought his ship close to shore and anchored there. The ship's boat was lowered, and Leif was rowed toward land. When he set foot ashore, Leif Ericson made history—without realizing it. He had reached the New World almost 500 years before Christopher Columbus made his first voyage.

The Norsemen found a barren, forbidding land. The ground was frozen and covered with great slabs of rock. Leif called the region *Helluland*— Flatstone Land. Historians today think this may have been either the southern coast of Baffin Island or part of the Labrador coast.

For Leif Ericson and his comrades, one trip ashore was enough. They saw that it was a hard place to try to live. So they rowed back to the ship and continued sailing—this time southward.

The second place Leif sighted was probably the southeast coast of Labrador. When he went ashore, he gave this flat, heavily wooded country the name of *Markland*—meaning Forest Land. Even though Markland looked like a place worthy of further exploration, Leif was eager to be on his way. There was more waiting for him. He had no doubt about this.

After two days of hard sailing, the Norsemen sighted land once again. They anchored and went ashore to spend the night. In the morning, they built small temporary shelters of sod and wood. Then Leif led his men out into the countryside to do some exploring.

It was a beautiful land with many trees. The grass was thick and green. Rabbits, deer, and other animals leaped and ran about in the forest. In a nearby lake there were the largest salmon any of them had ever seen. Leif Ericson called his comrades around him and suggested that they spend more time here. In the next few days, they set about building sturdy houses for themselves.

When the houses were finished, Leif called the men together once again. "I am going to divide you into two groups," he said. "Half of you will stay here at the camp, while the other half will explore the land. No one is ever to go so far that he cannot return by evening. And most important," Leif Ericson warned, "never become separated from each other!"

To people used to Greenland's bleak climate, this new country seemed like a paradise. Days and nights were of more equal length. Here, the sun was up when they ate breakfast and did not set until late in the day. The Norsemen talked about how easy farming would be here. The livestock could graze on the rolling grasslands and meadows of wild wheat. And nowhere had they seen signs that any people walked this fine land. "Truly," they said to each other, "luck goes with our Captain Leif!"

Then one evening, the explorers returned to camp and discovered that one man had not returned with them. Leif was upset. The missing man was his old friend, Tyrkir.

"We shall search until we find Tyrkir!" he called. Twelve men joined him and silently set out from camp.

They had not gone far when they heard sounds. Then Tyrkir himself appeared and greeted them. Leif was puzzled. "Why are you late, Tyrkir? How did you get separated from your companions?" Tyrkir pointed. "I saw something none of you saw. I saw something special. I found vines—with grapes growing on them!"

"Is this the truth?" Leif asked. "Of course," the old man replied. "I know vines and grapes when I see them!" Eagerly, he led them to the spot. Vines were growing everywhere, with bunches of grapes hanging from them. To the Norsemen, this seemed like a sign. Surely, they were meant to settle in this rich new land!

39

The next morning, Leif Ericson told his comrades that he had decided on a suitable name for their new country. "It shall be called *Vinland*," he declared, "after the many vines and grasses we have seen. That is a name worthy of the good things we have found here."

Some time passed before Ericson began to make preparations for the long voyage back to Greenland. He wanted a good cargo to take back with him. Timber brought high prices in barren Greenland. He had his men cut down trees and stack logs aboard ship. He also gave orders that grapes be gathered. The grapes were carefully packed into the small boat towed behind the ship.

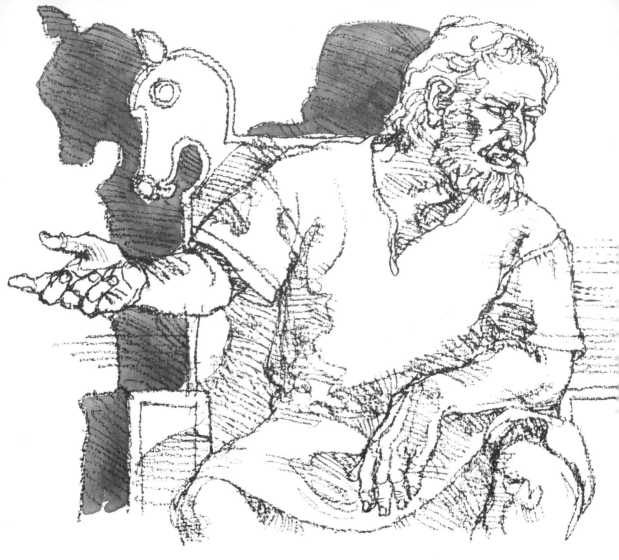

Then, Leif Ericson and his comrades hoisted sail
and left their Vinland camp. The winds were fresh
and favorable, and the return voyage across the
North Atlantic was peaceful. Several days later,
Greenland's ice-capped mountains came into view.

42

When Leif Ericson returned to his father's house, he was given a royal welcome. He sat in a carved chair beside old Eric the Red and told of his adventures in Vinland.

As the word of his great deeds of discovery spread throughout Greenland, people said, "Truly, he *is* Leif the Lucky!" To the Vikings, a lucky man was not only blessed with good fortune—he was also a man to honor and respect.

Leif Ericson never returned to Vinland, for when Eric the Red died, Leif became the ruler of Greenland. But Thorvald, Leif's younger brother, led several expeditions to the New World. It is said that the Vikings never settled permanently in Vinland because of trouble with the Indians, and that Thorvald himself was killed by an Indian arrow.

The complete saga of Leif Ericson is still to be told. A mystery remains. Where *did* he and those who followed him actually come ashore in the New World? Where *was* the place he called Vinland? Some people believe that it was in Labrador or Nova Scotia. A few think it was part of Cape Cod, or even Virginia. But most think it was probably a region of Newfoundland. It was here that ruins of a Viking house and fireplace, dating back to about the year 1000, were found. Perhaps this was the house of Ericson himself.

The son of a brave and daring adventurer, Leif Ericson is still remembered as a sailor of great talent and daring . . . and as the first European to reach the shores of North America. Even today, the sagas of Eric the Red and Leif Ericson are tales of great adventure.